DAWNING

To Margaret —
From Margaret,
with every good
wish.
Let me know when
your book is ready!

DAWNING

AND OTHER VERSES

Isabella M Hinchliffe

Matador
9 Priory Business Park,
Wistow Road, Kibworth Beauchamp,
Leicestershire. LE8 0RX
Tel: 0116 279 2299
Email: books@troubador.co.uk
Web: www.troubador.co.uk/matador
Twitter: @matadorbooks

ISBN 978 1784624 439

British Library Cataloguing in Publication Data.
A catalogue record for this book is available from the British Library.

Printed and bound in the UK by TJ International, Padstow, Cornwall
Typeset in 11pt Aldine by Troubador Publishing Ltd, Leicester, UK

Matador is an imprint of Troubador Publishing Ltd

CONTENTS

FOREWORD

I never set out to write, but the poems in this book came to me with ease. Some were inspired by talking to children, others just came. Many thanks to family and friends for their encouragement, and in particular, to those who provided the illustrations.

I M HINCHLIFFE
March 2015

SPOTTY DOGS

Spotty dogs are nice to cuddle,
But I dropped mine in a muddy puddle.
She was all dirty and very wet,
But I still love her as my pet.

TRAINS

Trains go through tunnels
And stop at stations.
They go to different destinations,
Like, Glasgow, London and even Oban.
They carry luggage in their guards' van.

MAISIE MOUSE

Maisie mouse has very big ears,
Big teeth, big smiles, and never tears;
Big eyes, big hands, and a lovely blue bow;
Shiny white teeth, all in a row.

WEE MOUSE

I'm a wee, wee, mouse
In a welly boot house.
I've got a little sister.
I call her a little blister!

PAWS

Paws, Paws, is my name.
Don't you wish yours was the same?
I'm quiet and sleek, and can be very meek.
But if you're bad to me,
I'll scratch, you'll see!

I'M SIX YEARS OLD

I'm six years old.
I'm very, very bold.
Nothing frightens me.
If a lion came by
I'd look him in the eye
And say,
"What do you want for tea?"
If he said,
"I'll eat you!"
I'd just say, "Boo!"
And I know he would run away,
Because I'm very, very scary
So he better be wary,
Or I'll catch his tail –
Then put him in Jail!

WHERE IS ELLIE?

Where is Ellie?
Watching telly.
Where is mum?
Playing the drum.
Where's Jaconelli?
Eating jelly.
Where is Pele?
In bed with a sore belly.
Where is dad?
On the iPad.
When's tea?
Half past three.

PLAYING WITH PAPA

Playing with Papa is so much fun,
Out in the garden, run, run, run.
A dribble, a goal, or even a fall,
It doesn't really matter at all.

He's always "up for it"
'Tho he's sixty six and a bit,
He runs out of puff a bit,
And likes to sit down a bit.

Then it's up again,
"Golf or tennis?"

I'm learning a lot,
And I'm getting taught,
That winning's not all
When playing with a ball;
But it's fun and it's teamwork,
It's losing with grace,
But still,
If I'm running,
I'm up for the RACE!

AJM

PENNY SKATER

Penny Skater was eaten by an alligator.
It was in the wrong water.
It should have been
In a pond or in a lake
Where is was much hotter,
Like in China or North America.

Instead it had escaped from a zoo,
And it caused quite a commotion
When it was seen in the Atlantic Ocean,
Following a ship.

Now, here's a tip.
It might have helped,
If Penny Skater
Hadn't taken the advice of a waiter,
To go and take a dip, from the ship.

There's no more to be said –
Now that's she's DEAD!

I WANT A PET

In my class we all want a pet,
But dad says we're not getting one yet.
There are lots of different ones –
A mouse, a hamster, cat or dog;
A budgie, a gerbil or you could catch a wee frog.

Four boys have got a cat,
Two girls have got a rat.
Six girls have got a rabbit,
With funny names,
Like Patch or Carrots!
One boy has got a snake; he keeps it in a tank,
But I've been to his house
And when you took off the lid,
It really, really STANK!

I've had two goldfish – they died.
I had one stick insect – I tried
To pet it;
But it didn't really need it.
It was happy with its hedge leaves
When I remembered to feed it.

My cousins, they've just got a dog,
It didn't come as a puppy.
It used to belong to someone else
And they'd taught it to do
'Keepie Uppy.'

They called it Lucky Lottie,
Lots of things she's learned to do,
Like, 'SIT!' 'COME!' 'GIVE A PAW,'
'LIE DOWN!' (that means sleep, to me and you.)

I really hope I get a pet.
They take a lot of care,
And it's always better, if it's a dog,
That someone's always there –
To take it walks, to feed it,
And I would do my share.
I'd play with it in my spare time.
We'd make a happy pair.

I haven't got a name yet
But I've thought up one or two.
The one that I like best of all
Is after that bear 'Balloo.'

If I ever get a dog,
I'll bring it round to show you,
And we can play at 'fetch the ball,'
And watch it run when I call –

But if I don't get one when I'm young
I've got a plan just in case –
I'll DEFINITELY get one when I grow up,
And live in my OWN place.

THE BUFFET
AND SLEEPOVER

Come to a Buffet on Saturday.
Come about 3 –
It's like a self-service tea.

There's going to be wee sausages, garlic bread,
Smoked salmon, maybe quiche.
It could be with broccoli.
I think you all like that.

We're going to drink Ribena, Capri Sun, water,
Badoit with orange juice,
And Papa and me
Will need a wee cup of tea!

And after that,
We'll have ice cream.
Food of your dreams-
Chocolate biscuits,
Smarties, fudge,
Mini magnums-
Your dads and mums won't mind,
Because it's like a party.

Then it will be playing,
Watching, dancing, carrying on!

Then bedtime,
Books that rhyme.
Up and down,
Running in and out the bedrooms.
Laughing, chasing,
Knowing we don't mind.

Until we say "ENOUGH!
I'm going to have to phone your dad
To tell him to come and get you"

But you know we're only kidding,
But you begin to settle down.

Then it's morning,
Time to get up.
Breakfast, cereal,
A piece of toast,
Yogurt, and for some now,
A cup of tea.

Then your parents come
To take you home,
And we're all exhausted,
Happy, delighted –
To have had you all to stay!

BUFFUT

Time 3:00
where Grandma and papa

BUFFET

S.R.M.

TRICKY RICKY

Ricky found things rather tricky,
And if he was tying a knot,
There'd be string everywhere,
Including the stair,
Into a fankle he got.

Ricky found things rather tricky,
And if he was baking a cake,
There'd be flour up his nose
And egg on his clothes
His mother would be very fraught.

Ricky found things rather tricky,
And if he was flying a kite,
The wind would it pull,
He'd fall as a rule,
And once he flew right out of sight.

Ricky found things rather tricky,
And if he was singing a song,
His voice would sound off,
Like a bear with a cough,
And each word would come out all wrong.

One day when he woke,
He said with a croak,
"I wish I'd get everything right."
His mother said, "Dear,
Don't worry don't fear,
All will turn out just fine."
And sure enough, it was just as she said,
And a change happened when he was nine.

As far as the knots,
At the cubs he got,
A badge to sew onto his sleeve,
For knots strong and neat,
To tie round a cleat
That would tie up a mighty big yacht.

Now cakes he could make
With never a mistake,
His sponges a sight to behold,
In fact he was good
At cooking most food,
It was eaten before it got cold!

Now flying a kite
Was a wonderful sight,
For Ricky the kite dived and swooped.
People would come
To have lots of fun,
And kite flying tips would be told.

Now Ricky could sing
Like a bird on the wing,
His song would fly to the sky,
So sweet and so clear,
So very dear,
It would bring a tear to your eye.

As Ricky grew older
He grew much more bolder,
And lots of adventures he went,
To the jungle, the desert
And places unknown,
With just a sharp knife and a tent.

Last time I heard
He was building a boat
The seven seas to sail,
To meet peoples new,
There'd be quite a few,
And maybe have rides on a whale!

SWEARING

Something they don't talk about
Are words you shouldn't use.
It's not until you've done it
That you'll be a bit confused.
You hear these words most every day
On the bus or in a movie,
And once they get into your brain
You might think they're really groovy.

One of these words I said, when I felt an awful pain.
It was the one where you 'take His Name in vain.'

Do you know what I'm sayin'.

Well mum jumped up, and said,
"Where did you hear it?
Not in this house, I swear it!"

They used to wash your mouth out
With water and with soap,
But that was when your mum realised,
The fact she couldn't cope.

There's other words that I now know
Some of them sound quite –
Well, how can I tell?
'Cos I don't know what they mean,
Except, well, 'hell.'

I don't think I'm going to swear –
There really is no need.
I know lots of other words to use
And plenty still to read. –
Like, Heavens! Crivvens! Help Ma Bob!
Golly! Blast! Gee Whiz!
These are the words I'm going to use
When I am in a Tiz!

I know that some folk will be pleased
That I have in the end,
Decided that words should not offend,
But that words should Mend,
Words should Care,
Words should Share.
Words should be Fair.
THEREFORE – NO SWEARING1

"DO YOU BELIEVE IN GOD?"

"Do you believe in God?" She asked.
"Why yes, I think I do.
I believe in everything that's very good for you.
Some know God in different ways,
The way their parents showed them,
But God is there for everyone,
Whichever way you know Him.

Some think God's a spirit, who lives within your heart.
It's there to help and comfort you, and help you do your part.

Some think God's a woman,
Some think God's man.
Some think they're right about everything,
But most do the best they can –

To understand what God wants of us,
To guide us on our way.
To help show Love to everyone
We hear or see each day.

God is Love. It's all around
So look about and find,
Let it live within your heart
And let it rule your mind.

Help each other everyday.
We're all God's children anyway.
Find the Love that joins us all,
Just open your mind, and hear it call."

MRS MCBOO AND
MRS MCSHOE

In a Glasgow flat
In a very nice street,
Lived Mrs McBoo and Mrs McShoe.

They were very tidy and every Friday,
They scrubbed and cleaned
Until the whole place gleamed.
They cooked and baked
Until their poor arms ached.
Then sat back and sighed
With a cup of tea,
And said to each other-
"A good job done.
Now let's have some fun."

So they played some songs
And it wasn't long –
Before they were dancing and singing,
The whole place ringing
With shouts of delight
And if you were passing at night,
You might get a fright,
To hear such a noise
From two ladies in a flat!

Now fancy that!
After an hour
They ran out of power.
They'd had enough,
They had run out of puff.
So time to relax
And rest their backs,
Eat their dinner
Always a winner – FISH AND CHIPS!

SORE HEAD

Do you remember Mrs McBoo?
The woman who lived in a flat near you.
Well, one morning when she did awaken,
A very bad headache she said she had taken.

As Mrs McShoe shooed her straight back to bed,
"A hot drink and sleep you need!" Is what she said.
Mrs McBoo, (who's very well read,)
Lay down with a 'hottie', and her little pink ted.

"This is the life." She thought with glee,
"I'll lie here and get up about half past three."
Unknown to her, Mrs McShoe
Was bustling about with a lot to do.
The shopping, the ironing all had to be done.
She always worked hard until half past one.

Mrs McBoo all warm and cosy
Crept out of bed to have a wee nosey.
Mrs McShoe looked all out and done,
She'd NEVER be finished by half past one!

Mrs McBoo then felt rather guilty
The headache was gone and now she felt frisky!
Into the shower, and on with her dress,
Soon she would help clear up all of the mess.

With a whistle and turn
She then did appear,
To Mrs McShoe who was standing quite near.

"You're fairy god mother now awaits!
Now lead me to those dirty plates!"

KNITTING

Remember our dear Mrs McBoo,
A hobby of hers was knitting to do.
Aran, Fair Isle,
She did the lot,
It all depended on what wool she had bought.

If a baby was born
A shawl she would make.
Although complicated, she ne'er made a mistake.
Her mother had taught her when she was quite small,
Before that she held the hank whilst mum rolled the ball.

'Tho nothing was needed
She never sat still,
Scarves, gloves, squares,
Whatever you will.

Sometimes she'd hear of a wee jumble sale
With stalls of home baking and sometimes old bales –
Of wool made of colours old fashioned and new,
With shades of a rainbow in every hue.

Down to the hall at nine o'clock sharp,
No need to tell HER to be up with the lark.
First the shopping, then a wee cup of tea
And a bit of home baking,
(That's cake, to you and me!)

Home to show Mrs McShoe how well she had done,
But SHE'D never found jumble sales much fun.
Together they'd plan how the day should then go,
And if it was raining, they'd take in a show.

THE HOLIDAY

The holiday this year for Mrs McBoo and Mrs McShoe
Was a Greek Island cruise ending up in Corfu.
The sun would be hot, the sea azure blue –
And time for sight–seeing,
Things old and new.

Up through the night, to catch a flight,
Packing being done up 'til half past one! (am!)
The mules, the trainers, the silver flip-flops;
Better throw in a pair of white socks.

The costumes for swimming
The jewellery for 'blinging'
The sun cream for applying
The books they'd be trying
To read, if not falling asleep,
On the lovely white decking.

No cooking for them for two whole weeks,
What a treat!
No cleaning, no tidying, no shopping to lift,
They could concentrate on buying a wee gift
To take back,
For their dear friend Jack.

At night they would dress in their very best
Of clothes newly bought, for weather quite hot.
In the lounge they would sit, and have a wee sip
Of the local tipple, OUZO,
Which could make them feel 'WOOOZO!'

Then off to bed with a very light head,
But ready next day
To be up and away –
For the next adventure.

There was nothing to censure,
Just two lovely ladies –
At home, and away.

THE MEXICAN PARTY

A big date was looming for Mrs McShoe.
She was no longer going to be just 'twenty-two.'
These days were gone.
A 7 and an 0, were the way to now go,
But – Hey Ho!

A special party was what was called for
And Mrs McBoo was planning a night,
And if she got it right,
Then she knew that Mrs McShoe
Would be de-light-ed!

A Mexican theme, that was the dream,
And such an event wouldn't make a dent –
In the budget.

When Mrs McShoe was out one day,
The Internet ready, then up and away,
Mrs McBoo had a field day.

She ordered chillies and cactus all made of card,
Sombreros, crepe ponchos,
A piñata, bright green,
Of a Mexican lizard,
The biggest you've seen.

The food would be easy
For already she knew
Some Mexican dishes
To name but a few –
Guacamole, nachos, salsa
Could be a snack,
Tortillas, camote,
She could manage that.
A bean stew, some salad,
And then birthday cake –
She was good at them,
Two maracas she'd bake.

Only two days to go
Then on with the show.
Twenty were coming.
The flat would be humming.
The feet would be drumming.
The tequila would flow.
It was going to be – a
FIESTA FANTASTICO!!

CHRISTMAS WITH MRS MCBOO AND MRS MCSHOE

When Mrs McBoo was well over two
To her auntie's in Glasgow she'd go,
At Christmas time – for a Christmas feast
As Mrs McBoo was her niece as you'll know.

Her auntie's flat was a sight to be seen
For auntie Flo did it up like a dream,
With tinsel and streamers and big golden balls,
With reindeer and Santas pinned up on the walls.
A REAL Christmas tree had the pride of place
In the bay window by the big fireplace;
Where it stood –
All decked up and fancy,
'tho just made of wood.

Now Mrs McBoo had her very own flat
With Mrs McShoe and a wee fluffy cat.
They'd shared it together for many a year
With seldom a cross word and seldom a tear.
And when Christmas time came
They were already prepared
For festivities and frolics
To which none could be compared,
For down to a tee they had got it at last.
In fact, in 'Christmas terms',
They were top of the class!

From out of the cupboard came boxes galore
Full of decorations that had been put into store,
And in every room
The lights would surround
The fireplace, the clock, the vases of flowers.
In fact it would take them hours and hours
To get it just right –
So to be perfect on Christmas Eve night.

Mrs McShoe was in charge of the food
And for months before it is certain she would
Have made puddings and cake and lots of delights
That would make you ecstatic the very first bite.

The cards would be written,
The presents all bought.
The food would be ready to go into the pot,
Then just before midnight
The doorbell would ring,
And off to the church with their friends they would wing –
For Christmas Carols they loved to sing.

If only snow would fall on Christmas Eve,
It would be the best Christmas they could ever perceive.

On Christmas Day
Their families would come, to have
Christmas dinner with their dear mums,
And after the presents, the games and all that
Their families would go, and they'd be left in the flat.

By candlelight, all warm and cosy,
The dishes all washed
They'd be tired and dozy,
But have time to reflect on a Christmas well done –
And already be planning for next year's one!

THE SALES

"Ah used tae say,
Ah'm no wan fur the sales.
It's aw rubbish onyway,
Whit they pit oot.

But noo ah'd agree,
Ah've hud a bit o' success ye see.
Ah got wan or two wee things,
At the sales.

Ah got a red dress for Chloe,
She's wan o' ma daughter's weans.
Ah got a lovely bag fur ma holidays,
Majorca this year.
Ah pure luv it ther.

Huv ye ever been tae TK Maxx?
They've got stacks
Of things that are nice,
At just the right price,
Fur me.

The thing is,
Ye kin always take it back.
They'll put it back on the rack,
For somewan else tae get.

See you an' me ,
We'll huv tae go tae Braehead,
Or into town, or maybe Silverburn.
Ah need a dress that could dae a turn,
Fur that weddin'.

Ok! That's a date!
Oh! Yer ma best mate!
See ya!"

'THE FLITTIN'

Read as a one sided conversation between two women.

"There's gonna be a flittin' – next door.
Aye, on oor floor.

How much were they wantin'?
Well, now yer askin'.
Less than they'd have got last year,
I fear.

Ther's been a lot o' folk lookin' and pookin'.

In fact there was this wan bloke,
She thought it wiz a joke –
He offered her money, aw in cash,
But she didnae like the look o'him,
So she said she had tae dash.

It's really quite excitin'
After aw the time I've been here.

Aye, ah know. That's right dear.

It's gonna need a doin' up,
'Cos the last time ah wiz in,
It seemed tae me that most of it,
Was ready fur the wheelie bin.

Aye, she's gonnae live next tae her son.
Naw, not Dan, the ither wan.
Ah think she's gonnae miss us
'Cos she's been here maist o' her life.

Naw, she's his second wife!

Ah wonder who we'll get in?
Ah hope it's no too many.
Remember we'd a cludgie in the stair
And we went there tae spend a penny.

Ah'm ready fur a change ma sel',
But my man's no for budgin'.
Ah ken masel', ah'll just huv tae keep on nudgin'.

Ah'll probably be carried oot,
Feet first in a box,
'Cos aw ma memories are here,
The good wans and the knocks.
D'ye want tae come in fur a cup o' tea?

Aye, there's wan comin' at half past three.
We'll huv a wee look out
Just you and me.

Aye!
Ah think ah'll start chargin a fee!" (Laughs)

THE EPIPHANY

She said, "You've had an Epiphany!"
Ah didnae know it wiz happenin' tae me.
It felt quite strange, to see,
To feel a bit o' clarity
Efter aw these years.

'Ave takin' tae writin' it,
All of it down.
Ah feel a bit of a clown.

Before ah had been feelin' –
Quite down.

Then, Ah had this 'Epiphany'
And a big bit o' "Oh Ah See!"
Ah now know it's up tae me,
Tae pass it on.

Efter the 'Epiphany.'
Came the 'Catharsis',
Ah had tae look it up
Tae find oot whit it wiz.

It said,
'Purification of emotions through art.'
Aye, it's a fact!
Imagine me havin' that!
Ah feel great now!

DOLLS, CLOTHES AND OTHER THINGS

There are lots of clothes I can recall,
Right from when I was very small.
They must have been important.
It started with my doll.

I loved my doll – Rosebud.
A baby doll, with baby clothes
Knitted by my mother.
She had matching sets of
Dresses with pants,
Coats with hats,
Bootees, mittens,
My old shawl, a blanket
And even some vests!

My mum's friend, she could sew.
She made Rosebud dresses.
I had quite a few
And Lyn had too.
(She was her daughter.)

I painted Rosebud's face
With nail varnish when I got some.
I gave her rosy cheeks,
But I spoilt her.
I gave her to my daughter,
Her limbs were hanging off.
I'll need to ask her,
If she's still got her.

My memories start with 'hand me down' clothes.
I had lots of those.
The first to mind was one of a kind.
It was a white party dress,
Organza, with a sticky out skirt
And pink flowers through the material.
I was about four,
And my mother said,
That Billy said – about me –
That I'd break a few hearts when I grew up.
That's the first compliment I remember,
And I was flattered.

My mother knitted all the time,
And some of it was fine,
But I'd have liked now and then,
A new BOUGHT jumper!

However I liked the fuzzy wuzzy boleros,
The cardigans, with wee flower things down the front.
She made me ones with
Mohair, Fair Isle, aran sweaters,
They were all the rage,
And she sometimes 'took in orders '.
There were sleeveless pullovers
Fisherman's knits, with oiled wool,
For my father.

She made beautiful baby shawls
With, what was it
One, two-ply wool?
They were soft
They were light
They were sort of off white,
And she hand washed them,
And pinned them out
On a sheet when they were finished;
Before being wrapped in white tissue
And given away.

But back to 'the hand me downs.'
I had three main sources,
And it mattered who they came from,
Because some were to my taste,
And some were not!

Lyn and Muriels', theirs were good.
I remember two school dresses, yellow and blue
Which I loved.
They had full skirts and wee puffed sleeves,
And when I could wear them, I knew that it was summer.

The worst 'hand me downs'
Were from my mother's friend-
She had two daughters,
And she dressed them both the same.
So I just outgrew one dress
After wearing it all summer long,
First with the hem up,
Then with the hem down –
And then I got the next size up.
So that meant wearing the SAME dress
For at least four or five years.
It seemed endless.

I had trench coats, a nap coat,
A duffel coat as well.
I had a swagger coat, a duster coat, a poncho.
And in my teens
I bought a brown suede coat
From C&A.
It was fitted – and complimented.
That felt good too.

When Lyn got her dress for the qualifying dance
Her mum said she would make me one
When it would be my turn.

Her dress was stunning.
It was all that it could be.
It was ballerina length,
With net underskirts
And a red velvet bodice
With a 'sweetheart neckline.'
Mighty fine!

She was like a princess
From a storybook.
It was quite a look,
And I thought that
Three years later
It would be mine.

But it didn't happen.
Fashions changed-
I didn't get that dress,
For some reason I don't know.

Instead I had to wear
A knee length aqua coloured,
Satin type dress,
With sequins at the neck,
With white ankle socks.
I wasn't pleased.

It's hard to believe,
But when I was just eleven
My mother said,
"I'm never going shopping with you again!"
I must have been difficult to please.
I had my own ideas.
We never could agree on many things.
(In retrospect,
I might have been a bit spoilt!)

She used to give me £5
I think it was about that,
And I'd come back with a skirt and jumper,
Well pleased.
My friends' mothers didn't allow that.
But mine did.
It seems strange now.
I wouldn't have done that to my daughter.

My mum was not a conformist.
She had her own ideas
And stuck to them
Which sometimes was quite hard.

But I realise it's been liberating.
I could experiment,
And express myself as well.

I had every fashion in my teens.
I was quite daring
But I didn't know that back then.
It was just for myself.

I had green nails,
White vinyl knee high boots
That had slippy soles
And I had to take them off once,
And carry them,
So that I could walk up a hill!

I was the first girl to get trousers
In our street –
Red ones like denim.
I loved them,
But some mums were quite shocked!

I wore pleated skirts, mini skirts, maxi skirts,
Bell-bottoms, drainpipes,
A white lace cat suit that buttoned up the back.
Like a James bond girl –
It got a lot of admiring looks,
But I didn't understand why.
At first I thought there was something wrong.
Had the stitching come undone?
But I had bought it,
So I had to wear it.

Clothes to me were
Something to experiment with, play with.
We didn't realise the impact
That some clothes could create.

Not like nowadays.
We didn't think –
'Sexy', 'pulling pants', 'see-through',
'Plunging necklines', 'sex appeal'.
We were relatively innocent.
'Tho now they will tell you that
The Sixties and Seventies
Were about drugs and free love,
But not where I grew up.

I loved that clothes era
Which was followed by
Thirty years of clothes taking a back seat to –
Mortgages, replacement cars,
Children's shoes, holidays,
Decorating, budgeting,
For all these years.

Now it's time to 'build the wardrobe up' again.
But it's so much harder as
The body's changed
It's got bigger, lumpier, droopier,
Stoopier and don't mention the derriere!
But what the heck!

In your sixties if you're healthy
You can throw caution to the wind!
Who does it matter too-but yourself?
ENJOY YOURSELF!
It's later than you think!

I've got the leggings, the jeggings,
The wedges,
The sandals, like children's Clarks
That we wore long ago.
(Mine cut out at the toe,
When they got too small.)

I've got the tunics,
Like the maternity clothes we wore
That covered lumps and bumps,
Of meals enjoyed,
And exercise – NOT employed!

I don't wear full skirts, stiletto heels.
I used to. I wish I could.
But now they are best seen on the young.

The girls now have got different looks,
Like dark and understated.
Outrageous, grungy,
The Forties Look.
Some simple, some classy,
There's many a bonny lassie-
Some grotesque, unflattering,
Unnecessary, to reveal all that flesh.
Sometimes it's more interesting to
To leave something to the imagination.

The bottom line is,
If you'll excuse the pun,
If you look good,
You'll look good in anything!
And by that I mean
Confident, individual,
Show self-respect
And cover up some bits.

Attraction's not all about the body.
There are beautiful eyes, genuine smile,
Being friendly, caring,
A person who is good at sharing –
Someone else's life.

Wear clothes for yourself,
Not to impress your friends or
The wrong type of man.

My advice is –
Be yourself.
Love yourself.
Respect yourself.
Allow yourself to feel good.
YOU'RE LOVELY AS YOU ARE.

MUSIC

"If music be the food of love –"

What does music mean to me?
Well let me see,
I seem to remember when I was about three,
Songs my mother must have sung to me, like
'Can I Canoe You up the River?'
'She Wears Red Feathers and a Hula Hula Skirt,'
'All the Nice Girls Love a Sailor,'
And the voice of Mario Lanza.

We had backcourt concerts;
Although for us it was back greens.
And all the children did a turn,
And I was told I was quite a stunner
When I sang 'A Gordon for Me.'

At school we had a folk song book
And I think we learned them all,
Like, 'My Love Is Like a Red, Red Rose'
'Cherry Ripe'
'The Lincolnshire Poacher' and 'Green Grow the Rushes Oh!'
Were but a few.
I wonder if you remember them
As well as I do?

We sang hymns every morning, without fail.
Our teacher loved them
And now I'm glad,
As always when times have been sad, or bad,
I've had words to comfort me, and make me glad
That she gave us all that to fall back on.

In the church choir we sang
'All In an April Evening',
'Handel's Messiah',
'How Lovely Is Thy Dwelling Place.'
And classics such as these.
I didn't realise I was learning music
That would always please.

I sang with friends for pleasure
To pass the time of day.
Jim Reeves, 'You're the only good thing that happened to me.'
We could harmonise, and it made our hearts fly free,
It felt good, satisfying,
And sometimes we'd end up crying.

I've heard Fifties, Sixties music
But the ones that I liked best
Were Elvis and the Rolling Stones,
And some of all the rest.

The first LP that I bought
When I got a record player was
'The Glen Miller Story.'
I'd seen the film
And I really liked it –
It put me 'In the Mood.'

I've been part of a chorus in musicals.
'Oklahoma',' Fiddler on the Roof'
To name one or two.

I love to go to concerts,
Almost anything will do –
Carmina Burana to Chuck Berry-
That one made me merry.
I was one of the first up dancing in my seat!

I like Desert Island Discs,
It's an education,
And you learn so much
About what music means to others,
We're all the same.

Music fills you
Thrills you
Fires you
Inspires you.
Moves you
Grooves you
Consoles you
Makes you come alive.

It 'Takes you right back to the track, Jack.'
When you hear 'The Rat Pack'
Down memory lane.

We wouldn't want to live without it,
In all its forms.
Country, Flamenco, Folk, Pop
Classical, Reggae, Hip-hop.

It can have
'The Voice,'
The X Factor,'
And you can
'Play It Again Sam.'

It adorns our lives.
It expresses, it fulfils.
Some songs stand the test of time –
'There's a song in my heart.'

EXERCISE

Now you know me better
It might come as no surprise,
That I don't really like – EXERCISE!

In the first decade it was easy,
You never stopped.

You were always outdoors playing.
Running, skipping, playing with dolls,
Playing with balls –
Bouncing, kicking,
Throwing balls against the wall,
Two at a time,
Spinning round, under your leg,
Behind your back,
With your friend.
There was no end,
Of the things you could do.

Chasing, cycling, sledging,
'Peevers,' 'Kick the Can,'
'Hot peas and Vinegar.'
'What's the Time Mr Wolf?'

Then in my teens and twenties
Dancing was my game.
I could have danced all night
And never come home lame.

The Scottish Selection –
The 'Gay Gordons,' 'Boston Two Step,'
'Dashing White Sargeant:'
In fact I knew them all.
'Strip the Willow' was the best,
When birling round with all the rest,
And never took a fall!

Oh! And the Ladies' Choice!
When you would get to choose the boys!

Then it was the 'Quickstep', 'Waltz',
'Cha cha cha,' 'the Square Tango'.
I never could do 'the Foxtrot',
There was something not quite right
About the rhythm of it for me.

The 'Twist', the 'Locomotion'
It could cause quite a commotion
If you collided with another 'training' couple.)
The 'Jive,' the 'Moonie'
The 'Shake,' the 'Slosh' –
There were hundreds, Oh Gosh!

I've been to classes for Keep Fit
Zoomba, Line Dancing and Step,
All prancing about.
I'd loved to have gone to Ballet,
Pointing toes, pirouetting,
Leaping and flying – through the air.
I could have been a dy – ing swan.

But I chose the twin dolls' pram instead.
(It was a financial decision.)

I've tried Yoga, Walking,
T'ai Chi,
Video Tapes, DVDs,
Energetic housework, the Gym.
What's left? –
For me to become DEFT.

Now grandchildren have come along,
So now there is no need
To care about 'taking up' Exercise.

It's all there, and I've done my fair share of
Changing nappies,
Pushing prams, carrying them about.
I've played Hide and Seek,
Coaly backs, "I need a carry."

I've been on a bike again,
Disco'd, been tickled;
Carried lunch boxes, school bags,
Raincoats, picnics and wet wipes!

I've exercised my lungs,
My tongue,
My body,
My mind,
I've done all kinds.
In fact, this writing alone,
Has been an Exercise!

HANDS

BACKS

Hands on
Hands off
Hand back
Hand –me-downs.
Handprint
Hand made
Hand cooked
Hand sewn
Hand-le
Handy man
Hand over
Hand picked
Hand stitched
Handy work.

Backhand
Off hand
Open handed
Left hand
Right hand
Handmaiden
Underhand
Hand on your heart.

Back door
Back to front
Back garden
Back green
Back ground.

Back off!
Back pack
Back peddle
Back room.
Back seat
Back up
Backwards
'A backie'
Back to the future!

Hand back
Play back
Outback
Redback
Lean back
Half – back.

Stickleback
Tail back
Wave back
Get back
Look back
Back line of the chorus.

MY iPAD

He's having to listen to me
At half past three in the morning.
I brought him a cup of tea
But it was plain to see –
He'd rather be asleep.
So I picked up my iPad
I'm really glad I got it.

It's great if I'm awake early
Or up late,
As I don't need the light on,
To see.

I can read the news,
Read reviews
Play a game
E-mail a friend.

Make lists
Look up recipes
Meanings of words,
Go through family photographs.

It opens up a new world to me,
When I visit the World Web!

I've influenced one or two
That they should too,
Including my sister-in-law, at eighty two,
Get one.

She thinks it's great
That although she doesn't get about the same,
She can see and speak to her sister,
'Tho they live sixty miles apart.

I never need be in the dark
I can find it on the Net.
Subjects like fashion,
Education and inspiration.

Programmes that you've missed,
(He likes the weather best!)

The children like playing the games,
Watching a programme,
It helps to calm them down –
And give you a rest.

I don't think, in the future
I need ever be lonely.
I can always 'talk' to whom I like.

They were very helpful in the store
When I needed – more information.
They simply explained, they understood –
The needs of the older population.

I'll always need real people,
Life events, like theatre,
Cinema, meals out,
Walks on a nice day.

But it's magic having the iPad.
I wish I'd had one –
Long ago!

ARCHIE McDIVOT

The weather for some will set up their day,
Especially for golfers getting ready to play.
Archie McDivot was just such a man,
And Saturday morning needed a plan.
The weather was crucial to act as a guide,
Rainwear or sun wear, he'd have to decide.

The bag was set upon the floor
And there he stood at the wardrobe door.
"Does this go with that?"
He asked his dear wife –
The woman he'd loved for most of his life.

"Yes." She answered, with barely a glance.
In fact, truth be told, she seemed in a trance.
'Cos Saturday morning was always the same,
When Archie prepared for 'HIS Beautiful Game'

The T-shirt, the sweater, the waterproof set,
The polo, the sunhat and all of the rest.
Maybe he SHOULD wear the new thermal vest!

Shoes cleaned, bags loaded,
"Goodbye, I'm away.
Home about 5. Have a nice day"

At the Club, his friends arrive
Already talking about their 'drive.'
A bowl of soup or a bacon roll,
Ready now to face the first hole.

"Fine drive." "Great swing!" "A very good pivot."
"Pity about that whacking great divot!"

Archie is hopeful about his short game,
For several hours he had practised his aim.
It seemed to be going just how he planned it,
None of his friends could call HIM a bandit!

Eighteen holes later, he's smiling with glee.
Indeed he had finished up in the first three.
A drink at the bar, time for a natter.
Yes! Men do in fact enjoy the old 'patter.'

Home to Faye – dinner waiting.
All it needed was the plating.
A glass of wine, a read at the paper,
And then of course, not much later,
A sigh, a sneeze and then the snoring,
A Saturday night some might find boring;
But for Archie McDivot and his wife, Faye,
It was just the end of a perfect day.

After all,
Faye too had had, her very own way!

FOREARMS AND FACE

Forearms and face, one shade of the human race,
His body like another.
It's these short sleeves
In the summer when it's hot,
His face gets tanned,
But not –
His upper arms or body,
They stay the same.

Very white,
You can see them in the night –
Glowing – like it's been snowing.

But I wouldn't like to see him wear a vest,
Like some of the rest.
He's too old now.
But we've got a photo of him in a red one,
When he was about thirty-one.
He suited it then.

In winter his face starts fading,
And his forearms start merging
With the rest of his body.

You never get a proper tan here.
It's always the same,
Year after year.
A wee bit here and there.

It's merging now.
He'll look the same all over,
From October until June –
Then it's off we go again1

I DIDN'T UNDERSTAND
THEM THEN

I wish they were here now,
The parents long since gone.
I didn't understand them then
And most often thought that they were wrong.

I had a happy childhood,
Of that it is a fact,
But I wished them to be different
And now I'm ashamed of that.

I wanted mum to be fashionable
And stylish in a way.
I wanted a house well – furnished
And invite friends up to play.
I wanted them to be the same
As the others round about –
To say and do 'all the right things.'
Of that there was no doubt.

I wanted to be cuddled
And kissed perhaps each day.
I wanted to confide in them,
But that was not their way.

I didn't understand them
But perhaps it's now I do,
Because now I've lived a life as well,
And have some experiences I can tell.

I didn't understand them then,
War, poverty and death –
They'd faced them all,
But still they journeyed on.

They did their best for both of us
Generous and fair.
They showed their love in other ways,
And the fact that they DID care.

They taught us the best values
Of what was right and what was wrong;
To be truthful, kind and grateful,
(And even the odd wee song.)

The fact that we've inherited
These values old and true,
Explains how an old-fashioned upbringing
Can be very good for you.

I didn't understand them then,
I wish they were here now,
To thank them for their guidance,
And let them take a bow.

It's taken quite a long, long time
To lead me to this line,
But now what I must say is –
I'm glad that they were mine.

WHERE DID WE SIT?

There were only two soft seats
When I grew up.
They were for your mother and father.

Where did we sit?
I can't remember,
Around the square table
On wooden chairs,
Or on the floor?
No, they'd have been a draught
Under the door.

We would all want to be near the fire
On a cold winter's night,
Then your front would be warm
And your back would be frozen!

At New Year,
If you were having visitors for their dinner,
You had to borrow chairs from the neighbours.
They all did it,
Carried them across the street –
That wouldn't happen now –
You would probably just eat it off your knee.

They say it didn't matter then,
What you had,
But it mattered to me,
Because it seemed to me that we had less
Than most of all the rest.

But now I realise we had what REALLY mattered.

I DON'T LIKE ALCOHOL

I don't like alcohol,
I guess you'll wonder why,
As it seems to be the apple in everybody's eye.

I hate the way it changes the people that you care for,
And makes them act in other ways
And forget that you are there – fore,
My mother planted in me the fear,
For her childhood was tainted by a glass of beer and whisky;
And to her home, sorrow it brought,
And that is why to us she taught,
"Don't drink! Don't be lead!
Think for yourself instead!"

A miner and a sailor's life
As a young man my father knew,
And the perils of drink were obvious
And taught him a thing or two.
Many the men were ruled by drink, the rum, the gin,
It all helped –
To fade the thoughts of those now dead
Who off to war did go
Ne'er to return 'tho then they didn't know.

I did of course try once or twice
To 'have a drink', with some ice.
Rum and coke was the chosen tipple
And soon I was dancing on the table –
A stagger back to the hostel then,
Vowing never to do it again.
A drink was spiked another time
In a simple glass, with some red wine.
Flying then was my first thought,
And out on the balcony I got.
Fortunately, with friends right near
It ended, without a tear.

The advice I gave to my offspring
Was loaded with fear and dread.
But fortunately they did display
Common sense – so no dismay.

Don't let others change your mind.
People will say all kinds of things
To make THEM FEEL BETTER,
If in your hand they place a drink.
It makes THEM think, that you'll be happy,
But remember 'Tam', and keep off the 'nappy.'

A glass of wine, with a meal I now take,
And have found another make
Of something I often find handy,
As a wee night cap,
It's a CHERRY BRANDY!

RELIGION

"What religion were you brought up in?"
It's a leading question,
And it seemed to matter a lot to some.

We were Church of Scotland,
And every Sunday we went to
Sunday School, Bible Class.
We joined the Brownies or Boys' Brigade,
Then the Church Choir.

A girl who lived beside us,
She was a Roman Catholic.
To me it sounded magical, mystical,
With candles, incense, ritual,
And she had to eat fish on a Friday.

We all played together,
Then when she went to secondary school,
She didn't play with us anymore –
That was another mystery to me.

You sometimes heard things like,
"He married a Catholic."
In a hushed tone,
Like there was something wrong.

When you were eighteen,
You were supposed to
'Join the Church.'
You'd have been in
The Youth Fellowship,
And EVERYBODY did it.

But not me!
I couldn't.
I realised I didn't understand it at all.
I was questioning
And I grew a bit apart.
I nearly broke my parents' hearts.
They said,
"You're supposed to be like a child,
And have FAITH."
I didn't marry in a church
But that's another story.
I put the whole question aside
And got on with my life.

I can't explain it,
And it seemed to be a coincidence,
But from then on,
Most people that I met, and got on with,
Turned out to be Catholic,
And it seemed that I could see with them,
More eye to eye.

Religion didn't seem as important, defining.
We could accept, question,
Share similarities.
Realise what was important,
Like family life, empathy,
Love for one another.
We had openness.
We developed the understanding –
That we were all God's children!

I've seen selfishness, ignorance,
Hypocrisy,
In some of the most 'religious' people
And in some non –religious –
I saw God by His other name –
LOVE.
Acceptance.
Love for your brother, your sister, for one another,
Regardless of their creed.

Now I know more about some religions,
Hinduism, Islam, Judaism,
Buddhism, Mormons,
Jehovah's Witnesses,
To name but a few.

Most think they've got the right answer,
Know the Way, the Truth and the Light.

Unfortunately I don't know people of these faiths personally.
There is no way to get together,
To be open with each other.
To learn from one another,
To dispel fear and ignorance.

I don't know.

I've had my doubts, my ignorant acceptance,
Disbelief, wondering,
Questioning,
Couldn't concentrate, conclude,
So I left it well alone.

I now think,
It's what you're taught.
It's how your parents viewed it.
That's where you start your stand.

You've got to find out for yourself,
If you can be bothered, be interested,
Feel the want to know.

'Religion' can offer
Guidance, Comfort,
Inspiration, Fellowship.
Something to put blame on,
To be thankful for,
To make life seem more purposeful,
To be a vehicle for good work.

'Religion' can divide friendships, families
Marriages, communities, countries as well.

We really don't know very much,
But we can all decide,
That what ever our differences,
We can search for the common thread –
Like,
Respect for one another,
Love for our brothers, sisters, and our fellow men.

You don't need to look to the leaders of religions
For all the right answers.
Look within your heart.

"How would YOU like to be treated?"
With respect, dignity, acceptance,
Empathy, be offered friendship,
Live with an open heart?"
As long as it carries the message,
Peace and Love to All.

Keep Love in your mind.
Let it lead you in everything,
You won't go wrong.

You don't need to understand it all,
Just know God/Love is everywhere.
Carry the message.

It will guide you,
Keep you right.
Just Love one another.

FEAR

Fear of failing,
Illness, no caress.
Fear of the past
Fear of being found out.

Fear of not being good enough
Slim enough
Tanned enough
Light enough,
Fear of not looking like the rest of the world.

Fear of the outcome
Fear of being over looked
Of making a mistake
Of not coping.

Fearful of the future
Of the unfamiliar
Of not being understood.

Fear of poverty, alcohol
Losing your job,
And all the rest.

Fear of relationships
Of getting too close
Of being hurt

Of being let down.

If you can,

Let it go – the fearfulness!

We are all the same.
We all experience it at sometime.
Some don't recognise it,
But it is better to be aware –

Then you can work at
Changing it, challenging it,
Living your life without it
(But be sensible as well.)

Search out like-minded people.
They'll help you to feel more
Confident, accepted, reassured;
And you can help them too.

Don't expect it to disappear overnight,
'Tho it's possible,
It might.

"IN THE LEAFY SUBURBS"

"It happened in the leafy suburbs,"
That's what they write,
When writing about 'nice' places
Where it's relatively safe to walk at night.

Well, I live in the leafy suburbs
And I know that some might think,
That people like me,
Who've had some choices,
Don't know about living life on the brink.

If I'd been born in my parents' time,
I'd have lived up a close
Or in a mining village.

It wasn't so easy for the last generation.
Life was harder then,
But lucky for me,
My parents understood
The value of an education.
That was the great decider,
Of how your outlook might be made wider,
If you got one –
An EDUCATION, that is.

But like me, wherever you live,
You'd probably agree-
That where you live,

Should not define you
Confine you
Design you
Or malign you.
Just be you –
Wherever you're from.

THE INVITATION

They're getting married – at last.
I thought weddings were a thing of the past.
They've lived together,
They have everything–
And now of course
They want the ring,
And 'bling.'

Everything's perfect,
They've had to save
To get all they want
From cradle to grave.

No need for dishes, the bedding and that,
They've got all that they want
Piled up in their flat.

The venue's a castle.
"They'll see to the hassle.
Just come and have fun.
We'll talk to you when the photos are done!"

Is love just a sideline to this main show?
The future's not certain, so who is to know?
For better or worse is quite a big deal.
I'm hoping and praying that this love is for real.

CHRISSIE

The Chrissie I knew
Was always very true
To herself, and all those who knew her.

She was always kind,
And you would always find her
The same way.

She always made you welcome
And 'tho things might have been tough,
There was always enough –
Steak pie to go round.

The family was the main thing
That she obviously held dear –
And it's fair to say,
They were the nearest to her heart.

She had a life you'd dream of,
With a husband, good and caring,
With children, and grandchildren
That gave pleasure, never wearing.

Chrissie, wife, mother, good friend, master baker,
Now you've gone to meet your Maker,
Always in your heart.

Although you are now apart,
You'll always still be here –
To those who love you dear-ly.

ANOTHER ANNIVERSARY

Another anniversary looming,
Time was just zooming past.
Did they think it would last?

It was more than forty years ago
When their love first started –
And decades on,
It was still full – hearted.

It was a rough beginning then
Her folks thought she could do better,
But it was written in their eyes,
And for them too,
A great surprise,
That such emotion could arise,
And they were certain.

She could confide in him
Laugh with him
Make love with him
Spend time with him.
Plan with him
Raise a family with him,
Criticise his driving.

She could nourish him
Support him
Need him, want him
Be annoyed with him
Argue with him
Wonder with him
Grow old with him
Remember the good times with him –
For better or for worse.

He could love her
Care for her
Share with her
Adore her
Explore her
Provide for her
Encorage her
Flourish with her
Try for her
Would die for her.
He could amuse her
Confuse her –
Put up with her moods.

He could listen
And not hear her
Even though he was right near her.
He could banish all the fear in her,
By being there.

Was it luck or was it fate
That they had found their best mate,
Their lover and their friend-
And there would be no bitter end.

Life was good, is good, and shall be good.

It wasn't all plain sailing,
A piece of cake.
There was some heartache.
Some fears, some tears –
But most of all,
It's been love –
In all its glory.
It's the old, old story.
Oh how lucky they are.

AN OCEAN
OF EMOTION

It started with a puddle
When she realised she was in a muddle,
Not shallow, not deep,
Just enough to realise –
She was getting out of her depth.

It swished and dribbled
As she carefully, paddled about.
Then the water got deeper
As it began to seep out;
Down the slippery slope,
Until she WAS out of her depth.

It grew from a stream into a river,
A torrent,
And she was being crushed as it came
Gushing, all around her.
It was difficult to hold on-
To keep a grasp of reality,
When life was moving past her,
So fast.

Then in a burst –
She was cast into an ocean,
Of overwhelming emotion,
Dark and grey;
It was carrying her away.

It seemed it would never end –
But then, with the help of a 'Friend',
She realised she was not alone.
Others had been in that water
When it was angrier and hotter,
And with time and trust,
She was told it would all calm down.

Some time later
The storm clouds cleared,
Sunlight appeared,
And she too grew lighter.

It came as a revelation
That after such trial and tribulation,
The world looked better than before.

The water was calm,
A sea of tranquillity,
Where all life lived and died,
As it was meant to be.

In the glistening haze
She was amazed
That all could be as wonderful.

No need to look down at a dirty puddle,
But instead, look to
The vast ocean of emotion –
And sail on,
Through the good times and the bad,
Try not to be sad,
Look for the silver lining.

I'VE HAD A BIT
OF CLARITY

I've had a bit of clarity,
Of mind, of thought.
It's only taken sixty years
To get to where I've got.
To realise what's important
In this world in which we live.
To care about each other,
To strive, and to forgive.

Forgiveness is a hard one
For some people especially so,
For life for some is so unjust
They've suffered a heavy blow.
But forgiveness lightens up the heart,
And lets us all move onwards,
Let God – in our understanding –
Be judge,
For it's little that WE know.

We must all be protected
From what's damaging and harmful.
The law should deal with all that's wrong
But show some understanding.
Our leaders should be honest,
Truthful in everyway.
They've chosen to be beacons,
And should honour us each day.

To you this may seem simple,
And you may have long ago –
Worked all this out in your own head
And be satisfied with what you know.
But I've just had this 'bit of clarity'
That's organised these thoughts,
And it's taken all this time
To get to where I've got.

DAWNING

I awoke one morning as day was dawning
My mind was all a glow
With words and thoughts
That filled my head,
Where they came from,
I don't know.

The need to get them written down
And clear my bursting head,
Was first and foremost in my mind
Before I rose from bed.

For several dawns as I awoke
The pattern did unfold,
As all my thoughts came tumbling out,
Some sentimental, some bold.

Where had these words arisen from
That came to me at break of dawn,
That let me see life like a light,
That now I saw shone clear and bright?

The clarity of rhyme and reason
Enveloped me, and cleared my head;
Revealed some wisdom and understanding,
That freed me from past time spent worrying –

Enough to have been given birth –
And make good the time we have on earth.